A Time of Crisis
A Time for Christ

by
Fr. Ralph W. Beiting
with
Tom Pelletier

*****

Fr. Beiting's previous CAP books include:
God Can Move Mountains
Appalachia...a Special Place . . . A Bridge of Hope
Promises To Keep . . . A Vision for Appalachia
Dreams of Faith
Called to the Mountains . . . The Autobiography of
Fr. Ralph W. Beiting
Frontier of the Heart . . . The Search for
Heroes in America
Pilgrimage of a Country Preacher . . .
A Journey to the Holy Land of Appalachia
A Family of My Own . . . The Dream
I Thought I Missed

Copies of these books can be
obtained by writing to:
Christian Appalachian Project
322 Crab Orchard Street
Lancaster, KY 40446-0001

TABLE OF CONTENTS

DEDICATION

I dedicate this book to those who instilled in me the knowledge that only Christ can answer a crisis. In particular I am indebted to my mother and father, Martha and Ralph Beiting, for allowing me to see the beauty and strength of Christ.

I am also deeply indebted to Mary and Joseph, the parents of Jesus; their prayers and example make Him so real and so important to me.

I ask both sets of my parents to watch over their child and help him grow in love and devotion.

More than forty years ago, Fr. Ralph W. Beiting was called to Appalachia to build church communities and ease the pain caused by poverty. In 1964, he founded an interdenominational Christian organization called the Christian Appalachian Project (CAP). By offering long-term, self-help solutions to the problems that hold Appalachia's people back, CAP gives the poor a chance to work themselves out of poverty and to see themselves as they truly are: the people of God.

CAP provides educational programs for children and adults, home repair assistance, business-development programs, elderly visitation programs, emergency relief assistance, and so many other efforts. With over seventy programs and activities, CAP brings hope and peace to those in need.

Through the generous work of thousands of volunteers, hundreds of local workers, and a host of loyal supporters from all over the country, CAP has become one of the largest relief organizations in America, and a pioneer in the development of programs to defeat poverty and inspire hope.

Prologue—The Challenge of Christ

I have just returned from a funeral. A classmate who was ordained with me in 1949 passed away this week.

There were six of us who were ordained that year for the Diocese of Covington, Kentucky. Now I am the only one left. All the others have gone to meet their Maker.

As I was driving home from the funeral, I could not help but reflect on the past.

I thought about the days in the seminary, when the six of us prepared for priesthood, and for service to people and to God. I remembered in particular how, in 1946, my class' second year of Theology, a new bishop came to our Diocese. He was determined to generate a spirit of enthusiasm for Appalachia, and for the eastern Kentucky mountain missions.

The bishop assigned several of us to spend the summer in that area. He instructed us to get to know the country, its people, and its opportunities as well as its difficulties.

I went reluctantly. My father had recently been in a construction accident, and his leg had been crushed. I felt I owed my family my services at that difficult time. Yet the bishop insisted it was my duty to go to Appalachia.

So I went—unaware that I was about to experience an extraordinary revelation.

I had grown up in northern Kentucky. We'd gone through the Depression, and through war, and had known great shortages and difficulties. Yet those hard times were no preparation for what I found in the mountains in the summer of 1946.

The war was over. Yet as America rejoiced, Appalachia was in despair. The war-time demand for coal was gone, and the young men returning from the service found no jobs waiting, no way to earn a living or raise a family.

That summer I watched an endless parade of rickety cars, as the young men left their beloved mountains in desperate search of employment.

Hope had disappeared in Appalachia. It was a time of crisis.

More than fifty years have passed since that troubled time. As I returned from my classmate's funeral, I could not help but meditate on all we had witnessed since 1946. I could not help but worry about the crisis we're facing now.

In the first decade after World War II, despair hovered over Appalachia—but there was hope beyond. There were jobs in Detroit. The national economy was booming. There were automobiles and appliances to build. The federal government was promising a better life for everyone. We all felt invincible, and utopia seemed only around the bend in the road, or over the next rise in the hill.

Today, in these closing years of the 1990s, even the federal government admits its defeat and failure. Welfare and the grandiose plans of the Great Society have not succeeded. We thought we could end poverty once and for all, but today it is more entrenched and more deep-seated than in the days of the 1950s and early 1960s.

What we see now is a new world, a global economy. The jobs that were once in Detroit, or Chicago, or other manufacturing centers in the midwest are now in China or Mexico or some other developing country. A great many good jobs and paychecks have gone overseas, never to return.

Besides the job loss from the global economy, coal mining has lost its power to create jobs. We still have coal mining, but mechanization has cut the workforce needed to a fraction of former times. Coal will never again produce jobs the way it did for more than a century.

There is no doubt in my mind that the crisis today is worse than when my bishop first sent me here fifty years ago.

I know the roads are better than they were then. More people have electricity. The schools are newer. Yet the future looks bleak indeed.

We have more children who are poor now than we did thirty-five years ago. More children who are abused. Even the federal government admits that the welfare system has created dependency, not freedom.

Our governor recently appointed me to the Kentucky Appalachian Commission. Each time I leave one of our meetings, I am saddened from all I've heard. For example, of the 750,000 people who live in eastern Kentucky, 59,000 receive Aid for Dependent Children. That translates into 25,000 families on welfare. If the parents have to find jobs under welfare reform, what are they going to do? Right now, it is estimated that our local economy can only provide jobs for about 800 of those families. The support system has been removed before a solution has been found.

In the meantime, our people are caught in the crossfire between the past and future. There will be many a tearful night and many a sad family gathered around an empty table. It will be a time of great misery for many.

In a recent pastoral letter, the Roman Catholic Bishops of the thirteen Appalachian states declared that we are truly at a time of crisis—and that something must be done in the name of Christ for the sake of the poor. But I wonder what we can do to arouse the interest and courage of our people. How will we get one group after another to say, "We are going to look after our neighbors here in our own land, and see what can be done"?

The other day I filled in for a priest in another parish. I learned from the members that despite the lock on the door, their church has been broken into six times in the last three months. Nothing was vandalized, but money was taken from the Poor Box and the Votive Offering. I don't know whether the thieves needed it for food, drugs, or alcohol. But I do know the system they once counted on is no longer there for them. I worry that we will see more of this kind of crime in the near future.

A few days ago, there was a knock on my door. There stood a man whom I have helped over the years. I had hoped that he'd get involved in construction because he had great skill in putting up drywall. He told me he was ready to start a business and even give jobs to two or three other people, but he had no money to buy the equipment needed to put up drywall. He asked for my help.

I agreed to buy him the tools, and hoped that someday he would repay me so I could help somebody else.

He thanked me and said, "I have a chance to do a job 150 miles from here, but I have no way to live there while I do. Could I borrow your travel trailer so my men and I could stay in it?"

I said, "All right, you may use it for the winter. But I'll need it for summer, because I bought it for the children at one of our camps."

In this case, here was a man of good spirit, someone willing to work hard, who really wanted to better himself (and in the process, give jobs to two or three other men!)—but there was no government program to help him out. He had to come to me.

Even when officials have the power to help people, they are woefully short-sighted!

Just last week I was invited to the site of a coal mine that had closed, costing 450 people their jobs. The mining operation had removed the top of the mountain, leaving about twenty-five acres of very flat land—a rare commodity in Appalachia. There were also several buildings on the site, including one with offices.

The mine owners hoped the county would take the

site over and use the facilities to create jobs. Yet when I arrived, I heard one man urging people to ask the county to decline the gift.

"If the county doesn't accept it, we can tear down the buildings and haul in dirt, and the federal government will pay us for land reclamation, and we'll have jobs," he said.

Yes—jobs that will only last a few months. Jobs that will tear down the very structures needed to produce permanent employment!

Then, after those few months, the people will come to my door, crying for help. This is just one example of why I fear that the crisis is only going to deepen.

What will happen to this land that I have come to know as my own? What will happen to these people who have become my own family?

As I drove back from my classmate's funeral, remembering all I had seen in the last fifty years, my heart kept asking those questions. It returned again and again to the same answer.

During the summer of 1946, when I was sent to Appalachia, one of the things I experienced was street preaching—which for me, a Catholic, seemed very strange indeed.

Growing up, I'd known preaching only in the setting of a church. It was part of the service. I had never seen preachers standing in open places—in front of court houses, or filling stations, or post offices, or general stores—proclaiming the Good News of Jesus Christ.

But at the end of my first week in eastern Kentucky in the summer of 1946, the two priests I was helping gave me the opportunity to do just that.

I don't think anything has profoundly changed my life as much as that preaching out in the open. It was like taking Christ out of doors—allowing Him to go beyond the sanctuary. Through the loudspeakers, the word of Christ raced through those valleys. His spirit climbed the hills and settled in the hearts of many people. That was a new and profound experience for me. What I learned was simple:

That Christ was for the marketplace as well as the sanctuary.

I also learned that He could heal a broken world as well as a broken heart.

Through street preaching, my world of spirituality went beyond morning and evening prayer, beyond the sacrifice offered on the altar, beyond the tolling of the beads of my rosary. I began to understand that all things had to be restored in Christ. He and He alone could bring about the change we sought.

I thought about Christ preaching at those roadsides of Galilee or Judea, reaching down to touch the sick and heal them, driving out evil spirits, even bringing the dead back to life—and challenging the minds of men to think about things they hadn't even dreamed they could do.

I thought about how He had said to the Apostles, "With Me you can do all things. Without Me you can do nothing." I had heard those words all my life. I believed them. But did I put them into practice in my daily life?

For the first time that summer, as those words of Christ echoed back to me from the hills, it seemed to me that we were reaching a deeper source of power and strength.

During my years in Appalachia, I have seen many noble efforts made by very decent people come to naught. I've seen people with worthy dreams leave in discouragement because they feel there is no hope, no way to make people here feel excited about the future.

There has been a vacuum, a hollowness at the core that has brought all their efforts down. The reason is that Christ was not in their plans. The great inner power was not there.

These days, we are told that God must be separated from our lives. We've expelled prayer from our schools. At Christmas we can't put a nativity scene on public property, even though the very essence of Christmas is the birth of Christ.

When counseling the poor and the troubled, the workers at all our state and federal agencies are not allowed to speak about Christ and the strong, vibrant, everlasting things of the Spirit.

This is the crisis that confronts us in Appalachia, and in America as a whole. This is the root of our sadness and despair.

The answer is to bring Christ back into the picture. To encourage our people to be greater than they are. To let them reach for the stars.

To let them understand they are the very image of Almighty God.

The solution to our crisis is Christ.

It is for that reason that I am calling this book "A Time of Crisis—A Time for Christ."

I hope to show that our problems result, more than anything else, from a lack of Christ in our lives, and how restoring Him to our hearts can heal all things.

The Family Often Broken

I've been working in Appalachia for the last forty-seven years. During that time, I have witnessed drastic changes in the family unit.

As a pastor, I have listened to the tales of woe of men and women struggling to establish families. As Founder and Chairman of the Christian Appalachian Project, I, together with the CAP family, have seen the disintegration of family life. More recently, as a member of the Kentucky Appalachian Commission, I have read statistics and heard predictions that are frightening.

I know that to end this crisis, we must bring Christ back to the family.

One of the things that bodes ill for families is the increasing number of children born to single parents. More than 10% of the men and women who live together are unmarried—unwilling to make a commitment to themselves and to the children they may have.

For those who do marry, the commitment is often

fragile. Divorce is one result—as well as a land of lost, unhappy children who don't know where they really live and with which parent they'll spend the weekend.

Other families stay together, but with little love. I remember counseling one couple. I asked the wife, "When was the last time you kissed your husband?" She could not remember—but it had been at least a year. Then I asked her "When was the last time you told him you loved him?"

"Oh, longer ago than that," she told me.

They were living together, but as far as I could tell, there was no love in that household.

I think one of the problems is that we have forgotten the spiritual importance of family. We are too involved with the material aspects of life—money, housing, education, or even health. These things are all essential to our existence, but they are not its meaning.

Another problem is our focus on the individual. So often we hear, "I've got to do my own thing. I've got to be me." We have become so self-centered. We have forgotten that our full potential is only realized in union and in partnership with love. We will never stand so tall as when we are part of a family.

When we study God's wisdom, we see that He has always used family to create His kingdom.

He created Adam and put him in the midst of a garden of pleasure. Yet Adam was unhappy. So God put a deep sleep upon him and created woman—and in the fullness of time, family.

Later, sin and sadness troubled the world. But God started again, with another family—Noah, his wife, their sons, and their wives.

Later still, God picked a young woman of Nazareth named Mary, and a carpenter named Joseph, and He brought them together in love. He said, "Will you help Me create a holy family? Will you, woman, give birth through the power of the Holy Spirit to a child who is My Son?"

The greatest treasure the world would ever see, the greatest hope it would ever know, came not through the roll of thunder, or the flash of lightning, or the sound of a great wind. It came through the simple quietness of family.

Then a marvelous thing happened. The Jewish tradition forbade the mention of God by name—it was too sacred. But when the Apostles asked Christ how they should address God, He answered, "Abba." Father. Or to translate "Abba" more accurately, "Daddy." We could call God "Daddy!"

Christ would make us mother, brother, and sister to Himself. He made us His family.

Even when Christ started His church, it was compared to the family of God. Through this family, He brought Good News for all the world.

There is simply no substitute for family.

In my own family, my mother and father had a great desire to love God and share their lives with each other to create a family. They trained eleven children to love God and love each other. Anything I've contributed to the world, I learned from my family. It has been my strength—not only my parents and grandparents and aunts and uncles, but my brothers and sisters as well.

How different things are today!

Late one evening a woman knocked at my door. "Father Beiting," she asked, "can I bring someone in? There's an old lady been standing all dejected on the bridge between Kentucky and West Virginia since this afternoon. I drove up and got her to get into my car a few minutes ago, to get out of the cold. Can you do something for her?"

"Bring her in," I said.

The elderly woman was confused and disoriented. I was able to learn that her husband had died, and she didn't know where her children were. She thought she had kinfolks in West Virginia. She'd been trying to remember where.

I got her a room in a motel. The next day our CAP workers began trying to find her relatives, to see if they would care for her. But for all practical purposes, we already knew the answer: this poor elderly woman had no family.

Another time a young woman told me she wanted to marry a man who lived a thousand miles away. They had never met—but they had fallen in love over the Internet! I counseled her that they should never marry before they had spent time together, face-to-face, and learn about each other's needs and differences.

I don't yet know how things will work out for them. But the tragedy of family life is that more and more often, this is the way in which I'm seeing young people go, rushing into relationships without thought to the consequences.

What can we do today to bring the love of Christ to heal the crisis of family? I think we have to start with the children. They have to see starting a family as the most momentous step they will ever take—not an escape or a selfish kind of gratification. They have to see something deeper in marriage.

One of the very first things I did when I came here was start a camp where I could reach the children and work with them.

Boys in Appalachia rarely give girls the respect they deserve—and this lack of appreciation persists into adulthood. The wife is always "the old lady" or "my woman." In our camps, we try to teach young boys that women and girls are a beautiful part of God's creation—and that one day they will be the partners of these girls, and become fathers who will care and give and suffer and share in the creation of life.

This isn't easy, because many of our boys have never known their fathers, or have been abandoned by them. They can't perceive of "father" as something good and lovable—as Christ knew His "Daddy." We remind the boys that often their own struggles are a result of not having a strong bond with their fathers. We tell them, "Please do not give that hurt to your children. Spare them what you had to suffer. Prepare now to be something worthwhile."

We also work with little girls—and sometimes have to fight the concept that men and women are competitors, even enemies. It is not so. God gave men and women to each other to be partners. We are different, men and women. We sometimes think differently. We have different needs and different strengths. But our differences do not make one right and the other wrong. Or one more powerful than the other. And there are so many ways in which we are the same.

This is the mystery of God's wisdom working within us, that we can complement each other.

What one doesn't have, the other does. In that marvelous way, family again is the answer to our problems.

We hope our boys and girls will grow up realizing they are made by God to be a part of each other.

So often, I find young people entering into marriage lightly, with no real preparation for this most important step.

The young woman with the Internet romance is just one example. I get so many calls from people wanting to marry on the spur of the moment. They call me on Tuesday and say, "Will you marry us on Thursday?" I answer quite sincerely, "No, I will not. It is not right for you to be put in such jeopardy without preparation."

At a recent meeting of our local ministerial association, I shared these thoughts. I said, "Wouldn't it be wonderful if we, the ministers of this county, would say to all who want to marry, that we will not perform the ceremonies until they have a period of instruction about marriage—about the beauty and also the difficulties of this holy union?"

I was pleased by their agreement. They liked the idea of being able to say, "This is the practice of all the ministers of our community."

Even with instruction, of course, there will be much for couples to learn after marriage. How do they adjust to one another? How will they adjust to children? What does it mean to be a good parent? How can you grow as a family? How can you love each other more as husband and wife?

In CAP we've founded a group called Partners that tries to help families who come to us for emergency assistance. The idea is that these problems result from a breakdown of family. So rather than just help the family pay the electric bill, or repair the leaking roof, we try to help them repair their family. We've had some exciting results and have been a source of Christ's healing.

In Partners and all of CAP's programs, we're trying to give people a picture of what God intends for them. God wants them to be partners working together with Him to form a holy family.

Another thing that would help make this happen is prayer.

I remind people that, "A prayerful family is a happy family." There is such power in prayer! If we would only pray that God's will be done and that His family will survive and grow, we will see wonderful things happen.

We must pray for that. I am convinced that family is the finest building block that God has ever given us to create a better world.

I am convinced that Christ's presence in prayer is

the way in which we are going to restore family life
to its fullest potential.

So join me, and pray. Christ is the answer to solv-
ing the crisis of family—the greatest crisis of our
time.

Let the Children Come

If ever there was a time of crisis for the little children Christ loves so much, it is now.

How different my childhood was from that of children today! I had a wonderful childhood, even in the worst of the Great Depression. As I've said, I was one of eleven children—and my father was one of nine, and my mother one of seven. Our extended family was very large.

I remember going to my grandparents' home every Sunday evening, and all my uncles and aunts and cousins would be there, too. My brothers, sisters, cousins and I played and got into all kinds of mischief.

Once a year, my grandmother and her four sisters would gather all the children in our family and take us on the paddle boat, The Island Queen. The boat would take us to Coney Island, a resort area upriver from Cincinnati. We'd go ashore for lunch, and then enjoy the amusement rides and all the things to see and explore. In the evening, exhausted but happy, we'd reboard the boat for home.

That yearly trip to Coney Island was just one of the family rituals that made us kids feel appreciated, like a special kind of people. But one day I overhead something that made me wonder if I was special at all.

My mother had given birth to four of her children within a span of seven years. I was the eldest. On this particular day, my Uncle Joe was visiting, and he didn't know I was in the next room.

"Maddie," he asked my mother, "don't you regret having had so many children so fast?"

For the first time in my life, I wondered, "Was I wanted? Was I part of a plan? Or was I simply an accident?" I held my breath, waiting for her answer.

"No," she said. "I wanted each and every one of them, and I pray that God will send me more."

I never let my mother and uncle know I'd over-heard them, but from that day on, I never doubted the importance of my life. I knew I was wanted, was prayed for, and had been joyfully accepted by my family.

Yet, how different things are today—not just in Appalachia, but all across this country. There is too little appreciation for children. People want things, not children. They want cars, houses, clothing, sports,

entertainment and travel. Children are pushed into
the background, the unwanted baggage of a materi-
alistic and secularistic society.

The word is being sent out clear and strong to
young couples, "Take care of yourself, don't let kids
interfere with your life, don't let them be a drain on
you—be careful."

So many families today have only one or two children. I think this causes problems for the kids. When
I was growing up, each of us saw all our brothers
and sisters as blessings. We learned to share, we
helped one another, and we saw how we were
strengthened by one another.

But today, only children come to me saying, "I'm
so lonely. Why can't I have a brother or sister?"

At times I hear them answer their question themselves: "I guess it's because my folks don't really
like kids. That's the reason they won't have any
more."

Of course, some only children are smothered by
too much attention. Time and again I've seen parents hover over an only child, doing everything for
the child, unaware they are not allowing the child to
develop and learn on his or her own.

The most terrible change in the way our society
regards children began twenty-four years ago—with
the Supreme Court decision called Roe vs. Wade.

Since abortion became legal, between 35 and 40 million children have been killed. This horror continues year after year.

Meanwhile, children are growing up aware of abortion, knowing that unborn children are being killed, and it frightens them indeed.

This violence carries over into their lives in another way. Just today I read in our local paper three separate stories about infants who were killed by their parents or their parents' lovers. A child is more likely to be killed in the United States than in any other industrial nation. This is tragic! This is the land that promised life, liberty, and the pursuit of happiness— and we are taking the most innocent citizens we have, the children, and putting them to death.

Not long ago I visited a man in jail. He had pulled the fingernails and toenails out of his infant son with a pair of pliers. Why? Because the baby's crying had made him angry.

I've also visited children in foster homes. They've been taken away from parents who have screamed at them, beaten them, or neglected their needs terribly.

Still other children are suffering in more subtle ways—through the neglect of their minds and character.

The children in our education system are not doing well, despite the fact that the United States spends more money on schools than any other nation on earth.

I wonder sometimes—how many parents still sit down and read books to their children? I suspect that too often they hand the child the television remote control instead. The kids can flick the remote and find whatever they want, from cartoons to things much worse. But they never learn to read.

Another thing I see in Appalachia—and I'm sure it's happening all over—is the way we spoil children. We just give in to them.

I grew up on a small farm, and we all had chores to do. My mother saw to it that we learned how to run our wringer washer, scrub floors, and help with the cooking and the dishes. My father saw to it that we fed the chickens, cows and pigs, and that we knew that we were responsible for these creatures that depended on us every day. We were being prepared for life.

Today, parents don't want to take the time to train their children or give them a value system or sense of responsibility.

Society tries so often to cure these ills by simply providing money and new school buildings and things such as that. We think if we just give children a computer or this or that, things will get better and peace and happiness will return.

The simple, fundamental fact is that to end this crisis we must put Christ into the lives of our children again. A child is not just a collection of atoms and molecules. It is a soul, a soul that needs Christ.

Christ was insistent on his love for children. When the Apostles tried to discourage mothers from asking Christ to bless their children—for the Apostles felt it had been a long day and their Lord was too tired—He said, "Let the children come to Me, do not hinder them; for to such belongs the kingdom of God."

So many of Christ's miracles involved children, such as the reviving of Jairus' daughter, and of the son of the widow of Nain. Children were always part of our Lord's love and concern.

Jesus wants very much to be involved in the lives of our children. Without Him, they will not find the love they deserve.

My goal, and that of our CAP family, is to reinstill Christ's deep love and appreciation for children into Appalachia—and our society at large. At many a camp fire at our summer camps, I've told children about Christ, and summer by summer, I've seen the children grow in His presence and become men and women of merit.

In the early 1970s, we set up child development centers for our younger children. These schools were a lovely way to remind parents, as well as the community, that children were the most valuable asset we had.

Our preschool teachers were excellent young women and men who came to help from all over the United States. They were not just dedicated teachers—they were deeply devoted to Christ. They exemplified what life with Christ could be all about. He was their joy, and the children saw it. With the spirit of Christ permeating the school, the children's lives changed.

We have also created Bible schools as part of our summer camps. Each summer since 1950, children have gathered together to learn the Scriptures and their meaning. They often put on plays about Bible characters. It's marvelous how the children understand the Bible, repeating its stories in their own words. Sometimes I think they even improve on the original! They translate the Bible into their own voices, their own actions, and their own lives.

Seeing these kids discover that God is not a stranger, not a disciplinarian, but a loving Father, keeps me excited and hopeful about their future here in Appalachia.

One of my favorite activities has been to take children on boat trips down the Kentucky and Ohio Rivers (in a way, recreating my own childhood trips on

The Island Queen!). We've watched the hills fade away and the broad river valleys stretch out before us. It's wonderful to see the faces of the children, as they discover they are part of a bigger land.

In a sad way, these boat trips help prepare those who must someday leave to find homes beyond Appalachia, because we have so few jobs. But our cruises also give us a chance to say to the children of Appalachia, "You are part of a big land. You are not alone. We are one nation under God."

In all of these activities—at our camps, at our child development centers, and on the rivers—we always pray. Mostly, the children pray in thanks for the beauty they've seen and experienced.

Sometimes they pray for the well-being of their families at home.

I know when they pray together, they are experiencing what it means to be community—to be a family.

One of my greatest rewards has been to see some of these children come back as adults, carrying their own children for me to bless in imitation of Christ. As I utter a prayer, give a hug, or mark the sign of the cross on a tiny forehead, I am reminded of Christ's love for us. Despite all our sins, despite all of the evils of the older generations, He is constantly giving us new children—and new hope.

Kenny and Brian are two brothers who once lived

next door to me, until they were put in a foster home because of parental abuse. I had formed quite a friendship with them, however, and at Christmas I brought them to my warehouse to let them each pick out a present.

They made a beeline for two bicycles.

As I was loading the bikes in the trunk of my car, I said, "Oh, I just remembered. I have some cookies inside. Would you like some cookies?" They rushed back in with me to pick out their favorite kinds.

When we came out again, Kenny, the older of the two, grabbed me by the leg.

He held me tightly and looked up into my face, "Father," he said, "thank you for loving us."

I will never forget that—a child calling out for love. Thanking me for love. Thanking the donor of those gifts, my wonderful CAP family, for love.

I think of Christ saying, "Let the children come to Me."

Yes, let us help them come to Him—for Christ is the answer. Only Christ, through the good work of others, can bring an end to this crisis among our children . . . and bring to them His love and joy instead.

Old Age—A Crown of Glory

I came to Appalachia when I was twenty-six years old. Now I'm seventy-three. In the long ago days of the late 1940s and 1950s, my thoughts about the elderly were far different than those that now fill my mind.

In the days of my youth, the elderly were considered special. They were the source of so many good things. We sought out their knowledge and wisdom. The elders were the books and pages of history. They told us the problems they endured and how they overcame them.

These were people tested by time, and refined by the grace of God. They spoke of God as if He were a companion, and encouraged us to pray and commit ourselves to a higher cause.

When we looked at the elderly, we knew we had no reason to be afraid.

My Grandfather Beiting was very special to me.

Our home was on his small farm. I helped him till
the soil, plant the seeds, and harvest the crops. I also
helped him in his carpenter trade. We walked many
a mile together to and from carpentry jobs, carrying
the tools of his trade, for he didn't believe in riding
the bus. It was so much better to walk, he said,
because we could talk.

At the worksite, each joint in the carpentry had to
be perfect. I remember helping him remodel the
church at our parish. There was a section behind the
altar where few people ever went. My grandfather
cut out a molding and handed it up to me to put in
place.

"How does it look?" he asked.

"It looks pretty good, Grandpa," I said.

"What do you mean, 'pretty good'?"

I said, "Why? It's all right."

"Let me see." He climbed up to look at how it fit,
and he said, "It isn't perfect."

"Grandpa," I said, "who in the world is going to
see it?"

He said, "You've seen it, and I've seen it, and God
has seen it. How many more people do you want in
on this? Do it right."

So we did.

Grandfather Beiting was also a great reader of history. He shared with me his love for America and his

spirited patriotism—and this was marvelous, considering he was only two generations away from the Beitings who had immigrated from Germany.

Grandfather also shared his incredible knowledge of the Church and its saints. His love for God was as genuine, and as much a part of him, as the soil he tilled, the boards he sawed, the books he read, and the miles he walked.

What greater gift could God give me as a youth than my grandfather, and the other seasoned ones who taught me and showed me the way?

How different it is today! Too often younger people discount the elderly. The elderly have become baggage, burdens on their way through life.

In the Appalachia I love, many young people moved away during the economically critical years of the 1950s and the 1990s. They are now scattered from one coast to another—and the elderly are left behind. I see them along the creeks where their cabins stand, and I know that the greatest sadness they face is loneliness, their lack of family, as they travel the final miles of their journey.

People say, "Well, they have radios and television to keep them company." But when I visit their simple homes, or their rooms in nursing homes, the television or radio is not even on. When somebody comes in and turns it on, thinking to be helpful, the elders pay it no heed at all. Their lonely thoughts are elsewhere.

Even more tragic, if possible, are the cases where the elderly have younger family members in the area who neglect them. The younger folks say, "Let someone else take him to the doctor." "Let someone else fix her roof or cut her grass." The worst of all is when younger generations take advantage of the elderly. Many of Appalachia's elders are on food stamps or welfare, and when the first of the month comes, their younger relatives come crowding in.

They take the elderly person to the store—and then they take part of his or her food for themselves. Or they take part of the welfare check as "compensation" for driving their elder to the doctor.

I think to myself, "How can they do that to the most sacred members of their family, the elderly?"

Then there are the elderly consigned to nursing homes. There is nothing inherently wrong with nursing homes. My own father was in a nursing home for more than six years before he died. But he never once missed a daily visit from a member of his family. He knew he was remembered and loved.

Several times a week, I visit nursing homes in our part of Appalachia. Often I am the only visitor some residents ever see. When I enter the room, they brighten up and reach out their hands. Even though they aren't members of my church, they are so eager to have someone talk to them about God.

Elsewhere, I see a growing fear on the part of many who are not yet old, but who already fear the anticipated loneliness and pain of old age. Why in the name of all that is holy should this be so? They worry about being a burden. They worry about not having the means to pay their medical bills, their mortgage, or the rent. They fear not having a car, and being stranded as the world flows coldly past them.

How contrary this is to the plan and hopes of God! God has always encouraged us to love and respect the elderly. The greatest legacies we have are the Ten Commandments. In them He stated firmly that we are to honor our father and our mother.

The great prophet Isaiah spoke the words of God when he said, "Even to your old age, I am He, even when you turn gray I will carry you. I have made, and I will bear; I will carry and will save." God assures the elderly of His presence. The Proverbs advise us that old age is "a crown of glory; it is gained in a righteous life."

God does not mean old age to be a time of punishment, but a time for importance, greatness, and dignity. When we fail to honor those who gave us our past, we are cheating our future. This is the tragedy. We act as if everything is of today, when in truth the past often creates the future, and if we have no love for the elderly who lived in that past, if we do not bring them into the whole of God's plan, then we harm ourselves more than we harm them.

As I move through my seventy-fourth year, this cause grows closer to my heart.

Often, when I am street preaching in an isolated village, older folks come out onto the porches. They sit and listen. Sometimes they even clap their hands and say, "Amen!" When I later thank them for their attention, they say, "Oh my, don't thank us, we thank you! You brought God to our homes. We can't get to church anymore, and a service on radio or television is not the same. You came, and you made it real."

I remember visiting one elderly lady on her porch. I thought I was doing good for her because I had brought her a little gift. But she said, "I shall pray for you wherever you go, and wherever you travel, that you may go with God, and that He may always be with you."

I thought to myself, "She has given me far more than I could ever give her!"

Over the years, the volunteers and employees of our CAP family have visited the elderly. We help them write letters to their loved ones, and we read the letters they receive. We give them the news of the neighborhood and what's happening across the creek. We take them to doctors, and we help them shop for groceries. But our visits always end with their request for prayer: "Won't you pray for me?"

This is the hunger they have, far beyond anything else. They want to know that God is in their house.

Of all the various activities we've had for the elderly, the one I appreciate the most is taking them out for boat trips on the river or a lake. For three or four hours, they see the beauty of God's creation and have an experience they have never known before. I also offer them a chance to steer the boat. They always say, "No, I can't do that!" Still, with a little coaxing, I get them to sit at the helm and take the wheel. I sit right beside them, direct them, and give them a sense of security. And steer they do. It's an adventure they treasure.

During the boat ride, we also have lunch, sing songs, tell stories of our lives—and pray.

So many elders have told me that of all the things we have done for them, what they remember most fondly is their time on the boat, sharing with each other, and enjoying God in His creation.

But perhaps the greatest thing we can do for the elderly is answer their many questions and concerns as the end comes near.

I remember Mrs. Murphy, whom I'd first met when she was age 77 and she asked me to baptize her. She became involved with many of CAP's programs, and worked like crazy for CAP all through her 80s. She was just amazing. In her 90s, she began to lose a little of her zip, and finally, at 97, she was dying.

I went to see her in the hospital and she said, "Father Beiting, what does God need with a 97-year-old woman who can't do a single thing?"

I answered, "Mrs. Murphy, you're not looking at things correctly. You can do a great deal for God."

"Like what?" she asked, surprised.

"Like loving Him," I said. "Telling Him you love Him, and asking Him to bless others, and to bless all the things that go along with your illness. You can say to God, 'You may have me. I offer myself up for the good of others.'"

With that, a look of peace came over her. We conversed a little more, and then I left. Later that afternoon, Mrs. Murphy died.

But I think she died fully aware that her last days were not wasted. God did have a need for her, and she was doing good.

So many elderly who are in physical pain ask me, "What good is pain? Why do I have to suffer so much?"

I tell them that Jesus said to us, the old as well as the young, "If any want to become My followers, let them deny themselves and take up their cross and follow Me." Through their suffering, they can help Christ in His redemptive work, bringing the world peace instead of hatred.

I've also met many elderly who are worried because during their prayers they become distracted and later realize they don't remember what they said. They worry that their prayers are therefore not worthy.

When I hear this, I say quite simply, "God knows you better than you know yourself, and He is pleased with you. He knows what you want to say. Your very desire to pray is the greatest prayer of all."

At other times I hear them say they are a burden to others. I remind them that they cared for their children, changed their diapers, and so forth, and did not think it a burden. "Now God is asking you to let somebody help you," I say. It is the way God brings us closer to one another.

As elders come closer to the Judgment Seat, they often begin to worry about the past sins of their life. I remind them, "All you have to do is tell God, 'I'm sorry, would you heal me? Would you forgive me?' That is enough."

I think Christ is still asking us to care for the elderly. We could offer a softer mattress, or a better pillow—or a hundred little things—but the assurance that God loves them is the best thing we can do to end Appalachia's crisis of the elderly. They may need material things and companionship, but their greatest need is Christ.

The Land—The Beauty of God's Reflection

I dread the coming of winter in Appalachia. Once the splendor of autumn is forgotten, and our hard-wood forests have turned to skeletons etched against a dreary sky, I can see the garbage that had been hidden behind the green of trees and underbrush.

Yesterday, as I was driving through the mountains to see an abandoned coal mine, a possible site for future jobs and housing, I was appalled by what I saw.

Plastic jugs and disposable diapers hung from the trees. Wrecked and junked cars lined the highway and tumbled into the creeks below, to join discarded tires, refrigerators, and stoves. At a wide spot in the road, people had pulled over and dumped countless loads of bottles, plastic tubs, and paper down the hill.

"Why," I thought to myself, "why must this beautiful land be abused?"

As I drove on, I saw an old bus parked on a tiny

bench of land. Smoke curled from a stove pipe extending out a window.

I saw old houses covered with scraps of metal. These scraps helped keep out the rain, but they also keep away any trace of beauty. I saw burnt-out house trailers, and others rusting away. The sight stained the hillsides. It was a disgrace.

My journey was delayed by a tractor and front-end loader that had stopped traffic. The crew was cleaning out a drainage ditch along the road. The ditch was so cluttered with trash that it could no longer do its job. After some time, the ditch was cleaned out and we proceeded slowly around the machines.

I had gone no farther than two hundred feet when someone in a car behind me threw a couple of empty cans and a cardboard carton into the newly cleaned ditch. All that effort, so quickly despoiled.

As I drove, I also saw the damage to the land caused by the unrestricted mining in the past. There are many sludge heaps, and erosion has taken its toll. New mining practices are more gentle, but we still face the challenge of how to put the mined-out land to good use.

Each morning before my work begins, I sit quietly and pray. I do so again after the day runs its course. I read about how God made all things, dressed them in beauty, and surrounded them with grandeur. I read of the beauty of the mountains, the purity of the streams, and flowers so magnificent that not even Solomon in all his glory could equal them.

God gave the task of caring for this beauty to our first parents, and through them to each of us. But God also wanted us to know joy. So He put beauty as a mantle over all creation.

Why has a world crowned with so much beauty, nobility, and purity been filled with such ugliness and blight? It is because Christ and His Father have been driven from our land.

People try to make things right, but I see much shortsightedness in their attempts. For example, the state puts up signs along our highways saying, "The next mile is maintained by Such-and-Such a group."

What is this really saying? It says, in effect, "Go ahead and pollute, destroy—someone will come along and clean it up. Just keep doing what you want, and others will try to make up for it."

We pick the wrong solutions in our attempt to improve things. We have to go much deeper. Better still, we have to go Higher.

I am convinced that only when we bring Christ back into our lives and our land, can we renew the face of the earth.

One summer afternoon, I took a group of children on a boat trip on a lake. We came to a point of land

and pulled in to let the children swim. When the children came off the gangplank, they drew back in dismay. Filth was everywhere: cans and bottles and diapers and junk.

"Ugh," they said, "we can't swim here, it's disgusting."

They were right. So much trash had been dumped into streams and carried onto the bank of this once beautiful lake, that it was tragic.

I said, "We will wait to swim until tomorrow. What we will do today is take plastic bags and gather up all this debris."

This point of land was not much bigger than a hundred feet long, but by the time we were done, we had fifteen large bags of trash.

The next day we came back. The children swam in the clear water and enjoyed the clean, sandy shore. They said to me, "We shall never throw anything into a creek or over a hillside again."

Before we left I said, "Let's take a moment to pray. Let's pray that this little piece of beauty you have all helped to restore won't be despoiled again. That it'll remain as it is today—a pleasant thing to see, and a joy to all."

For the past several years, the CAP family has encouraged the families of Appalachia to plant gardens in yards once saturated with junk. We give them seeds, fertilizer, and the encouragement to begin.

At the end of the harvest last fall, more than a hundred families gathered to review what they had done. One family told how their diets had improved, and how the children had vegetables to eat that the family normally couldn't afford. Another told how the family had grown closer as they worked together and spent time in the garden. The thing I enjoyed hearing most was a grandmother who expressed how pleasant it was to sit out on the porch in the evening and look out over the green beans creeping along the ground, the red of tomatoes on their vines, and the golden tassels of corn waving gently in the breeze.

"It makes me feel so good to watch over the yard," she said. "It's so much better than looking at junk. I go to sleep more sure that God loves me.

"This beauty is His reflection telling us that more beauty is still to come, when I see Him face to face."

With little things—a seed, a hoe, and a piece of land—we're saying to these people, "Let's make it beautiful again." In response, families tell me, "We tell God we're going to keep His beauty alive and well."

I know this is only a beginning. We have to work with other friends of the land, such as the National Forestry Service and our State Forestry Service. We bring representatives from these services to talk to children in our camps and youth programs. They explain how trees work. How they capture carbon dioxide and release oxygen for us to breathe—a miraculous thing.

We say to the young, "You are the stewards of God. God needs you, if there is to be true improvement and lasting beauty." If children can feel empowered by God to care for what He has created, then I think we shall see a change.

I'm especially intrigued by the potential of the land that was once home to coal mines. In one method of mining, the tops of mountains are removed to get at the coal, leaving flat benches of hundreds of acres. The land reclamation law says that once the mine is closed, the land must be restored. Sometimes this means planting trees, which is good.

But I wish some of these highlands could be turned into towns, with jobs and housing. If we can pull people out of the gloomy, damp hollows and up on to the mountaintops where they can see the beauty of a sunrise and the joy of a full moon, it will give them a whole new perspective on what it means to be alive.

Of course, problems will have to be solved first. How will we get water up there? How will we get rid of sewage? How will we acquire the land? With the mountaintop gone, the old property lines no longer exist, and legal battles are underway to redefine them. In addition, many land owners here hold onto their property with a tenacity unknown in other parts of the country.

We have to get the mining companies, the local land owners, the scientists and others to work together to answer these questions.

We need them to come together not only for profit, but for God. We need to say, "Let's be partners. Let's create a new Appalachia. Let's bring forth a new spirit of spring."

We have to bring Christ into it. Only Christ can overcome the selfish, the temporal, the material.

I have such hopes for this! There are literally thousands of these mountaintop acres lying vacant and unproductive.

I talk about my dreams with our college students. I try to get them to tackle the scientific and technical problems, and not simply accept the fact that there is no water there, or that sewage disposal is expensive. I tell them God has given them minds to be used— minds that can be creative to find new ways of doing things.

I talk to the business community as well. I say, "You have made so much money from this land. You have sent its resources all over the globe. Isn't it time to give something back for what you have received?"

I talk to our politicians as if they were ministers of God. They have the power to be His helpers in renewing the face of Appalachia.

Each day I pray that these men and women, as well as our landowners, our educated people, and our mining and forestry people see what a special calling they have to make the earth resplendent once more. If we can find new and exciting solutions for Appalachia, we can help other parts of the world where mining has taken its toll.

The other day I wrote an article for one of our major newspapers about the problems of Appalachia. I asked the readers for flowers, trees and seeds that I could distribute throughout Appalachia. With the help of these, I could change the face of the earth.

I would start with each little hollow and say to the people, "Here are some seeds. Put a flower box on your porch. Plant something in your garden. Make your home a thing of beauty."

If we can create small pockets of beauty, a kind of contagion may take over. People will see beauty and they'll want some, too.

I'm hoping the paper will print my request for flowers and seeds, and that its readers will become allies of my CAP family, who have already been so helpful.

My greatest ally in all of this is God and His Son.

"With me you can do all things," Jesus said. He reminds me, "Ask, and it will be given you; seek, and you will find; knock, and it will be opened to you." I know I do not walk through this land alone. I have never felt alone in Appalachia, or that I had to solve the problems by myself. I knew that He was with me, and that He always creates beauty.

This is a time of crisis for our land, and a time for Christ. We must come out of the bleak, ugly winter I now see through my car windows, and come into the clean, new beauty and promise of spring.

To all people I say, "Come, let us sing the glory of God. Let us invoke the power of God. Together, we can do it."

It is a powerful thought: Together, we can be the force of a new creation. We can return to this planet the beauty of God.

Prosperity and Poverty: The Legacy of Coal

Daniel Boone brought the first settlers into Kentucky. They settled Appalachia's valleys along the creeks and rivers, and made their living from the land—hunting, gardening, and raising farm animals for milk, meat, and eggs. They made their own clothing from hides and flax, and hewed houses and furniture from the native trees. There were a few general stores that carried goods from the outside, and every once in a while a peddler would wander through. But for the most part, the people were self-sufficient—and content.

Then coal was discovered in Appalachia. The cities of the East needed coal to make steel, railroads, and all the new machines of the Industrial Revolution. By the turn of this century, a new phenomenon dotted the valleys: the coal town.

The coal town provided new homes, schools, stores and hospitals. The railroads arrived, and on them rode new mine workers and families from the southern states and from Europe, Eastern Europe in particular. Where only a dozen years before, rural families had lived in quiet solitude, there were now towns with populations in the thousands.

By the standards of the time, the coal towns were well off. They had running water, paved streets, and even paved sidewalks. For entertainment one could play a round of golf, see a movie, or swim in the community pool.

The men who worked the mines were fairly well paid. They received some of their wages in cash, and the rest in script that they could use in the company store. Life was good and the earth was generous, yielding coal, oil, and gas just about wherever one set one's drill.

The people of Appalachia were proud to mine the energy that brought a victorious end to the First World War.

Prosperity followed prosperity, until that tragic day in 1929 when the stock market crashed. The Great Depression descended like an awful pestilence. It would test the souls of many Americans, causing heartache and hardship, but it was particularly cruel in Appalachia.

The demand for coal was down, and the mines were idle. Because there was no other industry to support the people, they began to leave Appalachia in great numbers.

Then there was another war. While it brought terrible destruction to much of the earth, this war nevertheless brought back some of Appalachia's sense of prosperity. Coal was needed to fuel the war effort. Many of the exiles returned home. As the miners cranked out coal in unprecedented amounts, the hillsides were alive with the laughter of children once more.

After four years, the Second World War was over. The young men returned from overseas. They married and started families. But their joyful homecoming was short-lived. The reality of unemployment soon descended on the hills.

This second out-migration, underway in earnest by 1950, was to last more than twenty years. America had never before seen such an outpouring of people from one place to another. Not even the Great Depression could compare with this new exodus. Many counties in Appalachia lost nearly half their population. Homes and some mining towns were abandoned.

Then another world conflict began—this time over oil. When the Arab countries put an embargo on oil shipments to America, coal took its place. The price of coal rose from $6 a ton to nearly $60.

Suddenly everything that was black in Appalachia was gold.

People flocked back to the hills. They built new houses, bought new cars, paid off old debts. Utopia had come to Appalachia.

Then the oil embargo ended, oil became cheap again, and the price of coal plummeted. In the 1980s, despair once again covered the land like a winter fog.

During the exuberant years, there had been efforts to bring other industries like textiles and shoe making to Appalachia. But as the 1980s ran their course, even these newer jobs disappeared. In the new global economy, it was cheaper to move factories overseas than compete at home—especially when the Appalachian workers went on strike, demanding to be as well paid as their brothers in the mines.

By the time the 1990s arrived, more than a third of the families in most parts of Appalachia were below the federal government's poverty line. For many, welfare had become second nature. It was easy to see how one could make more money and be more secure if one didn't work. In all truth, a goodhearted nation was trying to help people who had fallen on hard times. But money and government intervention could not end poverty. Instead, they rewarded indifference and complacency at the expense of adventure and trial. They took away initiative and freedom.

This past year, the government began to realize its folly. Not only had welfare not solved poverty, in many ways things were worse. Welfare had to end or be severely curtailed. Work had to replace indifference, food stamps and welfare checks.

Now in 1997, in the first months of welfare reform, fear and uncertainty are everywhere. There are precious few jobs to be had. Where will people once on welfare find work, especially in Appalachia? Already we're hearing predictions of the biggest outmigration since the 1950s. The skilled and the energetic will leave, and the old, the very young, and those without skills will remain. As I write this, Appalachia faces its greatest crisis in fifty years—perhaps even in this century.

But as a Christian, I have to have hope. There is a solution—we just haven't looked in the right places. The answer is hinted at in our own Constitution, which states that we are a nation under God.

We can come out of this darkness if we will only walk with God.

I know the people of Appalachia still have enough skills and enthusiasm to work their way out of this morass, if only a Godly hand is extended to them. What I am asking God-loving people in all our churches and synagogues to do is not just donate clothing or food—these are quickly used up, and leave people dependent on the churches and other organizations. I'm asking them to help me start jobs. Not large industries, but small ones, where everyone has a part in the work and they can form a much-needed sense of community.

One of the things I've tried to do in my own small community in eastern Kentucky is to develop a ceramics shop. Several generous companies have donated molds and given us advice and training. CAP has purchased a building, made shelves, set up the equipment, brought in electricity and turned the operation over to the community. Now our people are beginning to create beautiful and useful things out of our native clay.

I've done the same thing with a printing press. Again, I was blessed with a donation, this time of an offset press. We found some people with printing skills, and now they've started a small plant across the Tugfork River in West Virginia.

Donated equipment also allowed us to start a silkscreening operation, where workers print all kinds of emblems and pictures on sweatshirts and teeshirts.

Recently a fellow said to me, "I hear you're trying to start jobs. I can give you a piece of equipment that makes plastic signs for businesses." Another opportunity to create something new.

One of the programs CAP started years ago was

an operation that made Christmas wreaths and sprays. Right now a gentleman wants to take over this enterprise and expand sales from 30,000 wreaths a year to 45,000. We have great hopes for this.

We also have a chance to be a part of a very exciting new concept in housing. A man contacted me not long ago about his plans to make economical, modular homes. He has proven the efficiency, durability, and cost effectiveness of his designs, and he's already shipped homes to Japan, South America, Haiti, and Canada. The homes are simple to ship and erect, and they are attractive.

My dream is to make 120 of these homes a year in Appalachia. I'll need the resources to buy the land for the factory, and to train people to build the modules. The gentleman in Florida can sell these homes all over the globe. How wonderful it would be if the poor of Appalachia could give shelter to the poor of the Third World!

But to do any of these things, we need to get our churches involved. We need their help, and the help of others, to raise investment money.

A few years ago I started the Mountain Economic Development Fund to help businesses starting up or trying to expand in Appalachia. The staff at the fund shares with these businesses the expertise they've gleaned from similar ventures, and they coordinate the resources of state and federal agencies as well. Through this organization, we've created about 140 jobs in just a year and a half. It's been a great beginning.

As I've said before, I believe the only solution to the crisis of our time is Christ. But He needs us to put Him back in the picture. He isn't going to work miracles the way He used to. He can feed the poor once again, but not by multiplying loaves and fishes. He will feed them through the jobs He expects us to create.

We need to say to the business world, to the scientific world, to the educated world, to our work-a-day world, "We *can* do this. We *can* accomplish this— but we need Christ." We must give ourselves to Christ and be His ambassadors. We must think as He thinks, and feel as He feels; cry as He cries, and love as He loves. We need to take Him into places where He has been long forgotten.

We don't need a New Deal or a New Frontier or a Great Society. What we need now are great people— missionaries, our ambassadors for Christ, called forth by Someone greater than themselves. One who calls, "Follow Me." One who calls, "Go into all the world and preach the Good News to all creation . . . and behold, I am with you always, until the end of the age."

Is there any limit to what we can accomplish if we walk with Him? Oh, I think there is hope to end our crisis, if we walk shoulder to shoulder with Christ. I know there is power.

All we need do to reach things that we've never dreamed of is say to Him, "Speak, Lord, your servant heareth."

So many young women and men drop out of school and start families of their own. CAP offers programs to help them bear such important responsibilities at their young age.

Strong family ties and a solid education are the keys to helping families rise above the poverty that has plagued the region for generations.

CAP offers a wide range of programs for people of all ages, at all levels of poverty -- without regard to race, religion, nationality, or disability.

Loneliness is a common problem for many Appalachian elderly -- but visits from CAP workers ease their burden.

Despite the scarcity of jobs, many
Appalachian people choose to remain in
the communities they love.

As part of its economic development program, CAP started producing Christmas wreaths back in 1968 in order to provide jobs for local people. Our wreath factory now employs 125 people each year during the fall manufacturing season.

CAP's child development programs help build positive self-images, an excitement for learning, and a spiritual awareness.

Our summer camps not only provide recreational activities, they also teach children leadership skills they can build on for the future.

Helping people find solutions to their own problems has been CAP's philosophy from the very beginning.

Community, or Controversy?

When I was a young boy during the Great Depression, there was always a pile of coal near the lilac bush in our side yard. We were not allowed to use it, however. Our growing family was poor and on welfare. But my father explained to us children that the coal had been donated by members of our church, and was there to be used by neighbors even poorer than ourselves.

I don't think I'll ever forget that pile of coal. It was a symbol of community.

It is February as I write this, and it is cold outside. Many yards hold coal piles and stacks of wood. But I wonder if community is here now as it was then. We are shrinking as a community, shriveling. I often read about cases where people are in trouble and no one comes to help. Perhaps they are afraid to be involved. Or they are too busy looking out for themselves.

One Sunday afternoon I was driving with a friend near Knoxville, Tennessee, when traffic unexpectedly slowed to a crawl. As we inched forward, we finally saw what was causing the delay: an old man was standing next to a car half off the road with a flat tire.

No one had stopped to help. The cars were simply going around him.

We pulled over and I walked back to the gentleman. "What seems to be the trouble?" I asked.

"I have a flat," he said, "but I can't use my right side and arm because of a stroke. I can't get the spare out of the trunk, or the jack to jack up the car."

"How long have you been waiting here?" I asked.

"More than an hour and a half."

It being a Sunday afternoon, I suspect many people in the passing cars had come out of church, and now were on their way home. But no one had stopped to help.

After the young man and I changed the tire, the old gentleman asked, "Why did you stop?"

"Because I'm a priest. Because I felt you needed me, and you are my brother."

He smiled at me and said, "I'm a Baptist minister. I've never had much affection for you Catholic people. I suspect it's because I didn't know you well. I'm sorry I harbored any ill feelings. I shall always appreciate what you've done."

I replied, "I did it because this is what family is about. This is community."

In recent years, I've seen the races fall farther and farther apart. We have less sense of community than at any time since the 1960s. There are demagogues on each side who are more interested in their own prestige and notoriety than they are in the good of their people.

We are tearing the family of God apart, separating ourselves into groups by color, religion, and nationality. Each group has a desire to get ahead at the expense of another group. Is that family? Is that community? I don't stand taller because I've knocked down my neighbor. Our race relations can't be resolved by law. They must be healed by Christ.

Someday we will realize that in God's family we are all one. There are no competing groups.

I've also seen our country being divided by wealth, with the rich getting richer, and the poor getting poorer. Right behind a little chapel I built in a mountain area is a home valued at three million dollars. The couple who live there put in improvements almost every month: a black top walking path, a gazebo, a decorative waterfall, and more.

Just around the bend are houses in such terrible shape, I can't imagine people living in them. I look

at the contrast and can't help thinking, "Why do we
need three million dollar houses? How much enjoy-
ment can we get out of that when there are people in
such deep need?"

Instead of community, we are building economic
ghettos.

I also see a lack of community between men and
women. When I was growing up, we recognized the
many differences between our mother and our father,
but we never thought of them at cross purposes. Oh,
sure there was an argument every once and a while,
but they were partners — helpmates, one to the other.
We kids understood that. There was never uncertainty
there.

But what a spectacle we see today! Men and
women act as if they are enemies of one another,
jealously protecting their rights. The real answer is
to have trust and confidence in one another, and honor
each other's God-given dignity.

A priest I know once asked me to celebrate the
Masses for a week in his parish, because he was fly-
ing to Texas to attend a wedding. But later he called
to say the wedding had been called off. The man and
woman, both in their thirties, each had careers and
some financial resources. As the wedding day neared,
their lawyers began pointing out all the restrictions
they should make in a pre-nuptial agreement, in case

they ever separated. It all became so complicated and demanding, the couple decided not to get married!

I thought to myself, "What in the name of all that is holy is going on in this world?"

We also see arguments between young and old. The young seem so confused at times. They play around with drugs, alcohol, and sex. Their music sounds terrible. The way they dress is awful. At least, that's what we who are older think.

Yet I hear so many complaints about us older folks. We don't understand. We're out of touch with the picture. We're nothing but a headache and a hangover from the past.

I recall street preaching in Pike County, Kentucky. I went to a little country store. Across the road about a dozen teen-agers were "hanging out." As I preached, they yelled and called out things to distract me. I simply ignored them. Eventually they quieted down.

When I was done, I crossed the street and said, "Hello."

"How come we didn't make you mad?" they asked. "We tried to drive you off, you know."

"Why?" I asked.

"Because we don't like older people."

"Why?"

One boy pointed up the road. "You see that tree?"

It was a lovely oak tree standing at the edge of a yard. "That's the only cool spot in these parts. We go up there to sit around and talk and sing songs, and the lady who owns it drives us away. She sics her dog on us. So we hate old people. They're nothing but selfish old folks who don't know anything and don't care."

Somehow, we must build community again.

As I've suggested before on these pages, the community of family—our most necessary community—is being shredded.

After family, the community we need most is God's Church. Christ intended us to be one in His Church, as He and the Heavenly Father are one. We are to forgive one another, love one another, and know that we are together. This is the dream of God.

But what have we done with this great dream?

People use the Bible to push others out. There have been as many wars fought in the name of God and religion as have been fought for power, wealth, and territory. There are thousands of different Christian churches, each claiming to be correct and the others false. We are not content to be right. We must prove the others false, and in some way silence them.

Once when I was street preaching, a gentleman threatened to shoot me simply because I was a Catholic—the first one, in fact, that he had ever met.

"I'm a patriotic American," he said, "and I just want you to know that I think Catholics are the worst evil this country has. If it takes shooting you to keep you from ruining my country, I'll do it."

I was able to talk him out of this particular conviction. But I think it shows how powerfully we can feel about a faith different from our own.

I know throughout the course of the past two thousand years many of my Catholic brothers and sisters have also been guilty of prejudice. We have not always loved our Jewish friends and neighbors. We have not always been fair to our black friends, to our brethren in the Greek churches, to our various Protestant communities, or the Moslem communities now growing in our land. We have not always acted as Christ instructed us to act. For that we need to ask pardon and forgiveness.

Today's religious community is fragmented in a thousand ways. We have allowed this community to be used as a source of prejudice and controversy. Can this crisis pass? Can we truly be one? Can we make love the ruling force in our lives? I cry out with all my strength, "Yes! This must be!"

The only way is to get back to basics. We must return to God.

There was a time not long ago when some felt God was dead. Then we said, "Well, He might be alive, but He doesn't care."

Now it seems we've entered a new stage. Where once we learned that we were made in the image of God, now we make God into our image. He is what we like. What we want. What we think.

In some mysterious way, each one of us says we know God's mind, and that God is acting through us. What we despise, therefore, is what God despises. We put ourselves before God.

We must regain the humility that once was ours. We have to admit we don't know all. We have to realize that without Him, we can do nothing. But with Him, we can do all things. The more we give away, the more we receive.

I was reminded of this the other day when I visited a gentleman of modest means who lives outside of Madison, Wisconsin. Like so many others, he has been a good friend to CAP and the Church for many years. I asked him why he had been so generous to me, a stranger.

He said, "You know, my mother instructed me from the time I was little that if I was good with the things God shared with me, God would care for me even more. I've tried to do that. I must tell you, I've been the gainer. I'm much better off now than I was before I started to give things away."

One thing we can give away is our prayers for the

good of others. Today I received a phone call with troubling news. A friend told me that a man I've known for forty-seven years has been sick with lung disease. The doctors have told this independent, energetic man that he must spend the rest of his life on oxygen, twenty-four hours a day.

In the same conversation, I learned that another friend has cancer—and only has a couple of months to live. When I saw him last, he was a healthy and vibrant individual.

What is my responsibility to these two men? I called my friend with cancer and told him that not a day would go by that I would not pray for him. That I would offer up my sufferings for him.

To my other friend, now on oxygen, I said the same thing.

That's because even though one of us is Italian, one is Irish, and I'm German, we're family. We're community. We take care of each other.

Each generation needs to take care of the other, too. If the young people do something fine, we older ones must let them know how deeply we appreciate it. We have to do the same for the elderly. Oh, we get peculiar as we get older. I know that. Yet we need to be encouraged and told that we have been a benefit and a blessing to the world.

Men and women need to care for each other as

partners and helpmates. God asks man to love his wife more than he loves himself—and He asks woman to do the same. If we could follow that pattern in all our relationships, think of the problems we could avoid!

We have to reach out to our religious brothers and sisters as well.

I'm frequently invited to talk with Baptist, Methodist, Presbyterian, and other congregations. They ask me to come to their Sunday services to share with them some of the work we are doing in Appalachia, so they can become brothers and sisters to us and assist us. Here, too, community becomes the answer.

One of my favorite friends is a Methodist minister. He once got up in a ministerial meeting and said, "You know, I want to confess to being an idiot. When the Catholic Church first came to this county, I thought it was some sort of terrible retribution from God. But ever since Father Beiting has been here, he has shared whatever he had with us. He has given us things we could not afford to get on our own. He has given us not only material things, but friendship. I just want to tell you how much of an idiot I think I was."

Another minister got up and said, "Amen. I say the same."

When we pull together, when we put aside our differences and care for each other as community, wonderful things can happen.

I know Christ will use our efforts of love and caring to bring a solution to our crisis. We so need a religious awakening. We need a clear vision of God. A vision of God as our Father, Christ as our brother, and we as family.

In a family, in a true community, when one hurts, all hurt. When one cries out for help, all answer. When one reaches out a hand in love, all grasp it and hold it tight in love.

We need Christ and community to end the crisis facing Appalachia, and the world beyond. I pray that we will work together, and welcome every stranger as a brother or a sister deserving of our care.

Our Lord tells us that when we welcome others, we serve Him.

"I was hungry and you gave me food, I was thirsty and you gave me drink, I was a stranger and you welcomed me . . . Truly, I say to you, as you did it to one of the least of these my brethren, you did it to me."

Leaders on the Road Less Traveled

My father was a committed Democrat and a great lover of this country. So naturally our radio was on in 1933, when the new President of the United States made his inaugural address.

I was only nine years old, but I still remember hearing Franklin Delano Roosevelt speak to the nation.

We were in the midst of the Great Depression, and fear and anxiety were everywhere. My family, gathered around the radio, listened as the President told us that all we had to fear was fear itself.

Years later, I was a theology student listening to another radio when I heard that President Roosevelt had passed away. Not everything he had attempted succeeded. But I had been deeply impressed by his leadership. Here was a man with polio, who was wealthy, who could have taken his ease in the seclusion of his Hyde Park home. But instead, he chose to lead, and take a road less traveled—and we're all a little better because of it.

In 1950, I came to Appalachia as a priest. One of the counties entrusted to me was Madison County, home of Boonesborough. Boonesborough was the first settlement for families west of the Allegheny Mountains, at the end of the Wilderness Road. Daniel Boone had cut this road through the forests of Tennessee and up through Kentucky.

Boonesborough was his second attempt to bring in families from the eastern coast. The first had ended in 1773, when his oldest son, James, was killed by Indians as the party approached the Cumberland Gap. The others in the group turned back, discouraged, and told Daniel to abandon his plans.

He persevered, however, and founded Boonesborough in 1775. Later, he led another band across the Mississippi River into Spanish territory, in what today is the state of Missouri. Later still, he wandered farther west and laid out the first 160 miles of the Santa Fe Trail, and the first 150 miles of the Oregon Trail. Daniel Boone's leadership abilities, and his vision of the potential of this country, equipped him to blaze the trails that allowed future generations to settle this continent.

As a young priest, I traveled along the same roads that Boone carved from the wilderness, and looked out from the same mountains he climbed. I, too, had a vision—not merely of what was out there, but what ought to be out there. I was determined that I, too, would be a leader in bringing about a new and better tomorrow.

When I review the history of Appalachia, I am thrilled by the stories of our early heroes and heroines: George Rogers Clark, Simon Kenton, James Herod, Davy Crockett, Jennie Wylie—all part of that frontier leadership that forged a new country and opened up the West.

Of course, there was Abraham Lincoln, whose grandfather had come to Kentucky with Daniel Boone. Here in Kentucky, Lincoln began the life that would lead him to the presidency, and grant freedom to us all.

In our century, leaders like Alice Lloyd and Jane Buchanan stood up for excellence in education. They came from the East, gathered the children of Appalachia around them, and inspired generations without end.

John Fee, the Baptist minister, founded schools and a college in Berea, in pursuit of equal education and social justice for all races. His leadership helped countless others attain heights they had never dreamed possible.

I once had the privilege to meet Mary Brecken-ridge, a wonderful woman from a prominent Bluegrass family. She founded the Frontier Nursing Service, which set the standard for an entire nation on how to care for expectant mothers. Her nurses traveled by horseback, by mule, and later by Jeep, into every outlying place where women were waiting to give birth. Without her leadership, countless numbers of infants would have died. As I listened to her tell me stories, I thought, "Here is true leadership."

I also had the privilege of repairing a mansion that was built by John C. Mayo, one of the early industrialists of eastern Kentucky. He was the first to realize that this was one of the richest spots on earth. The oil, gas and coal beneath our soil, and the timber on its surface, were a kind of wealth that few places could brag about. Mayo hoped to develop these resources in a way that would bring prosperity to Appalachia, and good to the rest of the nation.

There were times in this struggle when Mayo was penniless, but he refused to give up. Because he would not quit, his treasure is still being mined, drilled and harvested today from the hills of Appalachia.

Where are such leaders now? I have written of the crises facing our children, our elderly, our families, our communities, and the land itself. Jobs are disappearing, and the gaps between rich and poor, old and young, white and black, and religious denominations are widening by the day.

The only way to narrow these gaps, and one day eliminate them, is through leadership. We need heroic men and women to walk the road less traveled . . . to go beyond the ordinary, to persevere.

Yet it seems each day's evening news, each newspaper, brings a story of greed and selfishness. The Ethics Committees of both the U.S. House of Representatives and the Senate are constantly at work uncovering one outrage after another among our purported leaders.

In business, we've seen industrialists so bent on lining their own pockets that they ignore the well-being of those who depend on them for survival. Profits have displaced people in too many minds.

In our colleges, I suspect sports programs get a disproportionate piece of the educational dollar. No one questions the student athlete who drops out to accept an unbelievable offer from the professional leagues. Our children, watching, get the message that that's what college is for—to sponsor a winning team, and to make its players more money. Not how to train leaders.

Leadership has suffered even in our religious communities. We are increasingly a church of bureaucrats, forming committee after committee, and accomplishing little else. I don't believe God so loved the world that He sent a committee—He sent His only Son.

There are, of course, exceptions to all this. We are blessed with politicians, educators, business people, church men and women, and others who are true leaders, and we must praise them for their work. But we need more people to stand with them.

How do we get leadership to flourish once more? How do we create more heroes?

I am sincerely convinced that once we return to the greatest Hero of all time, Jesus the Christ, we will have the answers.

Jesus never settled for what was good for Him. He concentrated on what would help us. He was despised, rejected, spat upon, called a Satan, a sinner, even insane, yet He did not shrink from any torment, for only when He was lifted up on the cross would He be able to draw all people to Himself. He laid down His life for His friends. He emptied Himself, and became our servant.

That is the real test of leadership. Are we servants? Are we serving others?

Christ sought His Father's will. That was His whole being.

For us to lead, we have to understand Who has the power, Who has the will, Who has the design. That is God. Heroes, like Christ, are those who make God's will their own. Who strive to serve others rather than themselves. Who are willing to die for a heavenly cause.

Pope John Paul II is urging Christians of all faiths to find Christ now, as the millennium draws to a close. He urges us to re-read the Scriptures and find the best Leader the world has ever seen, and imitate Christ, by making His life our own.

Within those Scriptures, St. Peter also calls us to be leaders: "You are a chosen race, a royal priesthood, a holy nation, God's own people."

Yes, we are all called to be leaders in some way or another. We are asked to build on each other—and if we do, we will see grand things begin to happen.

In my adult life, I've made it a practice to spend at least fifteen minutes a day reading the lives of men and women who have changed the world. I want to see how they incorporated Christ in their lives. They lived in troubled times in ages past, as I live in troubled times these days. What made them special?

I urge everyone who reads this book to also read about the lives of heroes. The recurring story is one of leadership built on faith, an enthusiasm that refuses to die, and a hope for the future that is truly admirable.

I try to use every program that CAP provides to spread the stories of heroes. In our child development centers, we tell stories about good people who have done great things. In our adult literacy classes, we encourage students to read these kinds of stories. We do the same with the students in our General Equivalency Diploma programs.

In our summer camps and youth programs, we emphasize the importance of having heroes—real heroes, not sports figures whose only talent and commitment is to throw a baseball hard or run fast.

When we work with our families, and with our elderly, we try to show them examples of men and women of all ages who have had the power and vitality to accomplish great things.

Of course, not all leaders have been good leaders. We've seen leaders like Lenin and Stalin, Hitler and Mussolini, and a host of others who had followers and who did things that they thought would make them the greatest leaders of the world. But they did not build on Christ—they rejected Him. Instead, they built on the frailty of human ambition and greed.

I think it's interesting to note that ultimately, they all failed.

What more powerful argument do we need to understand that leadership creates progress and dignity and peace—*only* to the degree that it is built on Christ?

If we are to overcome the crisis facing us today,

we must have new leadership. As God the Father said, "This is my beloved Son; listen to Him."

Yes, listen to Him.

Ultimately, that is where our answer lies: in the leadership of Christ Jesus, our Lord.

The Material Crisis

In the first year of my priesthood, I met two women who made a lasting impact on my life.

I met the first one through her husband. They'd been married five years and had two children. One day the husband came to me saying his wife had gotten a divorce and was living with another man. Would I talk to her, urge her to come back to him and the kids?

A week later I happened to meet her on the street. I mentioned that her husband had asked me to intercede on his behalf.

She looked at me and said, "You must be crazy. I had nothing but hard times with him."

This surprised me. "Did he harm you?" I asked.

"Oh, no. Nothing like that. It's just that he had an ordinary job and we had to watch every penny and make everything stretch as far as we could. I was tired of being poor. Now it's all changed. Look at the clothes I wear now! I bought them new at a fashionable store in Cincinnati. Over there is my new car. My new man gave it to me. We have a servant to wait on us, and someone to clean house, and I can buy whatever I need."

"But what about eternity?" I asked. "What about the fact that Christ said we should stay with our married partner until death do us part? Aren't you afraid of death and what will come thereafter?"

She said, "I don't even think of death. All I know is what I have today, and it's all I've dreamed of. I have every material thing I want. I shall not give up this man to go back to a man who is poor."

The other woman that I met that first year had a disability and had to spend much of the day lying down. But she never complained about it. She never found fault with others. She was always trying to help those who were near to her.

She had been married for five years, and all during that time she had prayed for a child. I asked, "Would a child not complicate your life, your health? Would it be wise?"

She said, "That's not important. You see, I know how marvelous it is to be alive. I know what a wonderful gift God has given me. I want more than anything to give that gift of life to someone else, and give a child the beauty of knowing and loving God as I do."

Later she became pregnant, and had a difficult time. But when I visited her, she'd tell me not to worry. She was happy because of the new life within her, and she knew God had heard her prayer.

At last she delivered a fine little girl—but at a cost. Her labor had been long and difficult, and within a couple of days, this very special woman was dead.

Before she died, she told her husband how grateful she was that he had loved her, and loved her enough to let her give life. If she had to die in giving birth to this new life, she was happy, because she had shared the greatest gift God had given her.

This woman couldn't do all the things she would have liked to do. She couldn't dance, she couldn't play sports, but she could love life. She saw beyond the value of shining, glittering things and saw that the meaning of life was God.

Each of these women saw life in an entirely different way. The first looked only at the surface of things. The second looked beyond, to the core.

Ever since the Garden of Eden, mankind has had a hard time figuring out the material side of his world. Adam and Eve were tricked into thinking if they only took a material thing, an apple from a tree, they could be like God Himself. If they had just one more thing they would be happier, and greater than they ever imagined.

From that time on, the Western World has felt that if we can only have more and more, we're going to be happier and happier.

Of course, the world has also seen the opposite view—a view that says material things are wrong, or filled with evil. Throughout history, there have been people who declared that it was wrong to drink alcohol, or curl your hair, or go to a movie or dance. Some groups have even felt marriage was wrong. Anything that was from the material side of life was somehow suspect, and not really of God.

The real answer is not to reject the material world, but to make sure that the spiritual world is foremost, and that the material world is used to God's ends, not our own.

Our present time puts a great emphasis on the material. No other period in history has seen such a proliferation of material things. Advertisements and articles in the media constantly bring wonderful things to our attention, and tell us how much we need these items. We will be forever unfulfilled if we don't go out and buy this or that right away.

We have established a lifestyle that is impossible anywhere else in the world. To do all this, of course, we pay a price. We are convinced that everything is so necessary and important. We now have both parents working to pay the bills. We are in debt. We use credit cards when we are low on cash, and essentially pay for the same item again and again through the interest rates.

With all this consumerism comes tremendous waste. Our landfills are overflowing. Boatloads of garbage from our big cities drift from port to port, having nowhere to unload their awful cargo. The cities try to dump their refuse on the rural areas.

The wasted food! A recent survey said that the edible food that is thrown out in this country in just *one* day could feed a city of 60,000 people for a *year*.

When we look at entertainment, whether it's a professional ball game, a concert, a movie, or some other family amusement, we see that the prices have gone out of this world. It's almost impossible to take a family out for an afternoon of fun.

Then there is the growing cost of health care, now beyond the reach of most of the poor. A friend of mine just had an operation on his leg and it cost $20,000! That is more than he can make in two years.

But the most frightening thing about our modern materialism is the peer pressure it puts on all of us to spend, to spend, and to spend. I can't count the number of times I've heard my nephews and nieces discuss how they have to have this new pair of sport shoes, because all the other kids have them. It's not just the young people.

On top of the money we spend on material things is the time we spend on them. How much of our time do we think about them? How much energy do we expend in our efforts to get them? We have no spare time left to devote to anything, or anyone, else. How many parents are out there trying to get material things for their child, when all that child wants is some attention and a hug?

Some people resort to stealing to achieve the material things they desire. I remember a teacher coming up to me one day, saying, "Little Andrew is stealing. A bicycle is missing and the only person who was around was Andrew."

Andrew was a child I'd been helping, so I intervened. I went to his house and said, "Andrew, where did you get the bicycle I see in your yard?"

He didn't say anything.

I said, "Did you take it from that boy at school?"

He said, "Yes, I did."

"Why?"

"Because I'm the only one who didn't have a bicycle," he answered. "I didn't want to be different from all the rest, so I took it. That boy's parents can get him another one. They're richer than we are."

I thought to myself, "Is this what our materialism is doing to a little boy?"

Sometimes the desire for material things leads us

to the great vice of envy. As a consequence, we may want to ruin something special that belongs to another person, because we know we could never obtain it. How many times have I seen children break someone else's toy, simply because of envy?

Vandalism is another consequence of envy. People deface and destroy property in anger because they feel deprived.

The offspring of all this materialism is secularism—that frame of mind that reduces the world to the material, to things we can see, touch, hear or smell. Things that are of the Spirit are not part of this world, because they are not real.

In a secular world, prayer, sacrifice, charity, even God, have no meaning. When the divine is left out, tragedy is not far behind.

Another fallacy about materialism is that we look only to the material world for solutions—to money, power and prestige. We form committees, set up study groups, and make endless reports. We've seen this in government, in education, in industry, and even in our churches.

I think all of us want to make religion alive and dynamic. We want to see it produce good results. Yet how are we going about this? Right now the big issue is "inclusive language." We have to change even the words of Scripture, to make them "gender neutral" and impersonal. Then we're told that what we really need are new hymn books, because the old hymns are no longer "appropriate." Maybe we need new vestments or new robes for the choir, and a few more banners to display. If we get rid of all the old buildings and put up these startling new structures that reach up to the skies and are filled with glass, that will do it. Certainly all these things will bring people closer to God.

I'm sorry, but I have to smile at such things. The material things certainly have their role in our lives. But they are not the most important part, nor the first part.

We see this clearly in the life of Jesus Christ. When He was about to begin his ministry, the devil tempted Him, hoping to destroy Christ's plan for redemption. After Christ had fasted in the desert, He was hungry. The devil said, "If you are the Son of God, command these stones to become loaves of bread."

That would seem a clever idea in today's material world—if we can take a material thing and make it bread, that would be very fine, indeed!

But Christ said, "It is written, 'Man shall not live by bread alone, but by every word that proceeds from the mouth of God.'" He found His solutions in the spiritual world.

Then there was a rich young man who came to see

Christ and asked what good deed he must do to have eternal life. Christ told him to keep the commandments.

"All these I have observed," the young man said. "What do I still lack?"

Christ said, "If you would be perfect, go, sell what you possess and give to the poor, and you will have treasure in heaven; and come, follow Me."

We are told the young man went away sad, for he had many possessions, and could not bear to give them up.

Christ sought to change the world. How was He going to do this? By getting the Emperor of Rome to do one thing, or getting the High Priest and Sanhedrin in Jerusalem to do another?

Neither. He did it by filling men and women with love. He filled them with dreams and ideas, gave them the Holy Spirit, and sent them out into the villages where He was headed, saying, "Carry no purse, no bag, no sandals." He was going to change their world without any of these material things.

The same truth has come home in our own times. When Stalin headed the communistic state, he didn't care about spiritual leadership. He said, mockingly, "How many legions does the Pope have?"

Of course the Pope had no military legions. But the spiritual power of the Pope was enormous. He had prayer and the ability to remind the people of the Eastern Block that they were God's people and had God-given rights and dignity.

Materialism and secularism together form the most pernicious crisis facing us today. Unless we can see the whole picture—the spiritual world as well as the material world—we will never recover.

I have tried at every turn of the road to live the spiritual and the divine. When I first came to Appalachia, I had no idea how I would succeed and bring vitality to the mountains. I had no resources. I had no money.

Now, more than forty-seven years later, CAP serves hundreds of thousands of people. More than a thousand groups and agencies come to CAP to share the gifts that we've been able to collect through our wonderful CAP family.

All this came about because we were willing to go to God and put all our dreams in His hands.

Each of us needs to look at the world each day and realize that God is its creator. Each drop of rain, each leaf, each flower should let us know there is something even more beautiful. They are but a reflection of a greater beauty.

As I grow older, and see the children of Appalachia, I have hope for an end to our crisis. These new ones are younger than I. They will have the time to work for change for the good of all.

My only prayer is that they will not put all their energy into the material world. I pray that they, like the woman with a disability who so longed for a child, will look deep into the core of life and find the divine.

With Christ, I know they will be able to do all things.

I hope and pray that all who read this book will decide that they, too, will be part of the solution; that they will use the material world to build the greater, spiritual world. That they will end our crisis not by putting their courage and hope into the frail and the brittle, but into the sure and the true, which is Christ.

Hope and Faith—The Defense Against Cynicism

You can't go through a crisis without wounds.

For the last eight chapters I've been describing the crisis we're in. In this chapter I want to talk about one of the wounds that has resulted from this crisis: cynicism.

Our time is full of cynicism and it is a great tragedy of the American spirit.

Cynicism means moral skepticism and pessimism. It is a distrust of everything. It is contempt for the virtues and values of others.

It is a terrible disease. It is against everything God has told us. It is the absolute enemy of the Good News of Christ.

I was recently in a meeting with the governor of our state and many high officials in state government. There were also a number of private individuals, like myself, and an audience of several hundred people. The point of the meeting was to discuss the new changes in welfare and how to find new solutions to meet the needs.

I was shocked when one person after another in the audience got up and complained that the federal government wasn't doing enough, the state government wasn't doing enough, everything was unfair, and no one really cared.

I was shocked because there was so much distrust. It seemed that not one person in that entire audience believed that those of us on the panel were really there looking for solutions.

The lack of faith was just astounding. Cynicism had a hold of that group in a powerful way.

It was shocking to me because we were there precisely because we wanted to help. The cynicism only got in the way of finding solutions. It was extremely frustrating.

This problem of cynicism rears its head in many parts of our lives. When families come to me because they are having problems, I often ask them why they don't go to church. I try to suggest that asking God for help could be part of the solution to their troubles. So often I hear, "Oh, we don't go to church. You can't trust those ministers and preachers. They don't really care about people. They're just after money and glory."

Now, I know there have been scandals among

religious denominations and that there are a few
tainted apples. But I have come to know ministers
and preachers of all faiths and I find them to be, over-
whelmingly, an exciting and wonderfully dedicated
group of men and women. The bushel is healthy,
despite the few bad apples.

Yet cynicism keeps the pews empty.

I have also spoken with many men and women who
live together but won't get married. They tell me they
have no faith in marriage.

I remember a couple who came to me asking for
work. They led me to believe they were married. I
gave them work and things were going along
smoothly until I heard from another source that the
man had been married and was, in fact, still married.
He had a wife and three children whom he had abandoned.

The next day I asked the couple if they were married. They said they were. Then I asked the man about
his other family. He turned ashen and couldn't speak.
The woman looked at him with shock and anger. She
was completely unaware.

I asked him why he didn't marry her. He said,
"Because I don't like marriage. I don't trust it. It
doesn't work. My parents were divorced and my
marriage didn't work. I have no faith that it will work
with her, either."

Cynicism was destroying the lives of so many people—this man's real wife, his children, and now this other woman, who was terribly shocked and hurt.

Sometimes I talk to young people and try to convince them to go into politics or government. I tell them that it's an honorable way to affect our future, to help create a new world.

They look at me like I'm from another world.

They say politicians are just crooks and liars. I tell them of my own experience with politicians and that, again, with the exception of a few bad apples, they are mostly a dedicated, committed bunch. My own father was mayor of our town and my brother was a councilman and a county magistrate. I'm proud of the job they did.

But the young people have no faith. "Why are you so cynical?" I ask them. They look at me as if I'm crazy.

I recently talked to a group of young people about sex and the idea that they should wait until they are married. I was surprised by what they said.

"What's so special about marriage? Most married people aren't faithful, and fool around anyway, so what's the big deal about having sex before marriage? And people get divorced all the time, so what's so special? Why not just take what you can? Marriage isn't the promised land, you know."

Again, cynicism is poisoning lives.

I get the same kinds of answers when I ask people to stay in Appalachia and work on the problems. "Why stay?" they ask. "Why not just get out and start over somewhere else? Nothing will ever change here."

Not if everyone with God-given talent leaves, I try to point out.

All of this is the result of cynicism that stems from a lack of faith.

It is a lack of faith in people.

When I look at the history of America and of Appalachia, I see that over and over again, people rose to the challenges and triumphed. The people who settled this country faced enormous obstacles, but they kept going. The people who came over the Appalachian Mountains to find a new land faced unbelievable struggles, and yet they kept working and trying, again and again, until they found ways to make their lives work and build something new.

We have so many examples of people facing a crisis and finding the courage and strength to overcome. If only we would look to the past, we could overcome our cynicism.

The other thing that leads to cynicism is lack of faith in God—in His plan for His people.

If only we could fathom the depths of God's love,

the extent of his knowledge, and the universality of his wisdom, we would have no fear, no lack of trust. If only we would look to Him for comfort and hope, we could banish cynicism forever.

No one loves this land or its people more than God. The amount of love and time and beauty He has lavished on this land is truly astonishing.

No one knows this land or its problems and strengths like God does.

Most of all, no one wants to ease the problems and comfort the people more than our Father in heaven.

I used that word Father for a reason. Just as a father and mother want nothing but the best for their children, so God wants nothing but the best for His children, His people.

If we have faith, He will find a way.

So often, people say, "We can't do that. We don't have money for that. That won't work."

I say, "We just have to try and have faith that God will find a way to make it work."

There is enough money to solve every problem we have. There are enough people, enough skills. There is enough of all we need, if we just ask God how to put it together.

One day recently, a friend called to say that a man he was helping was in need. The man's car had broken down. My friend said this other man couldn't

continue his job without a car and he wondered if I
had any vehicles I could lend the man. Unfortunately,
I didn't. Yet . . .

I prayed about it and the very next day, I received
a letter from a woman in a nursing home in Cincinnati. She said she had a car, in good condition, that
she simply couldn't use anymore. She wanted to
know if I wanted it to help people in Appalachia.

I called her immediately, and thanked her and
prayed with her. We arranged to have the car brought
here.

How can we be cynical when God's world works
this way?

The other day, I received a call from one of the
men who volunteers in our Attic Stores, where we
sell used clothing and other essentials to the poor.
He told me that his health was getting worse and he
wouldn't be able to work in the store anymore.

That evening, I was worrying about how to replace
this wonderful man's work, when I saw a note to call
a woman in New Orleans who had once been a member of one of my parishes. When I called her, she
connected me with another woman who wanted to
come to Appalachia and volunteer. When I called the
second woman, she was delighted about the idea of
working in the Attic Store.

These kinds of things happen all the time. They

are signs of God working behind the scenes to help His people in Appalachia. If only we'd have faith, I know He could help us even more.

Jesus said, "Fear not, O you of little faith. I am with you."

He *is* with us. We do not walk these roads alone. We are never abandoned. We do not dream alone. We are connected to a power that we cannot even imagine.

I received a call not too long ago from a woman in Washington, DC. Her son had been running a small business making stained glass lamps. Unfortunately, he died suddenly and left no heirs and his property and equipment went to his mother. She read in one of my previous books that I had been trying to start a stained glass industry here in Appalachia so she called me.

She gave us all of her son's equipment and supplies. Hopefully, a small business will result from that. Maybe an entire industry will eventually grow.

Another time, I got a call from a man in northern Kentucky. He offered me a 24-foot box truck for moving clothing and household items for our Attic Stores. Another man called out of the blue to donate sign making equipment.

When things like this happen, how can I doubt? Why shouldn't I go forward when I can see that there is a great power on which I can call by simply asking.

If I were a cynic, I would never have asked. Or, I might have looked at these gifts with a suspicious eye and said, "No thanks."

Cynicism can kill so much. It is an insidious, dangerous force.

Faith, on the other hand, can move mountains. It is a joyful, constructive force.

Psalm 91, one of the most beautiful of all the Psalms, expresses how I feel:

> *You who dwell in the shelter of the Most*
> *   High, who abide in the shadow of the*
> *   Almighty,*
> *Say to the Lord, "My refuge and my fortress,*
> *   my God in whom I trust."*
> *For he will rescue you from the snare of the*
> *   fowler, from the destroying pestilence.*
> *With his pinions he will cover you, and under*
> *   his wings you shall take refuge; his faith-*
> *   fulness is a buckler and a shield.*
> *You shall not fear the terror of the night nor*
> *   the arrow that flies by day.*
> *Because you have the Lord for your refuge;*
> *   you have made the Most High your strong-*
> *   hold.*
> *No evil shall befall you, nor shall affliction*
> *   come near your tent,*
> *For to his angels he has given command*

> *about you, that they guard you in all your*
> *ways.*
> *Upon their hands they shall bear you up, lest*
> *you dash your foot against a stone.*

In Isaiah, God tells us what will happen if we put this kind of faith in Him:

> *They that hope in the Lord will renew their*
> *strength, they will soar as with eagles'*
> *wings;*
> *They will run and not grow weary, walk and*
> *not grow faint.*

I have walked these valleys and climbed these hills for more than 47 years. I had precious little to work with when I started, but great things have happened. I have not grown weary or faint. More and better things are yet to come.

This did not happen because of my strength or intelligence. It happened because I believed that He will raise me up on eagles wings and His angels will guard my every step. God will hold me in the palm of His hand.

No crisis can defeat that mighty hand.

Epilogue—I Shall Never Give Up

Though I am in my 74th year of life, I have no intention of retiring. I pray every day that God will give me the strength to continue working for His people in Appalachia until my last breath.

I know I will not reach the end of this work before the end of my time. I won't win the prize. Poverty will not be banished from this land.

I know there will be more setbacks. There will be frustrations and heartaches. I know I face many nights of worry and doubt.

I know the people of Appalachia will not be completely free. Children will still be abused, women slighted, the elderly lonely.

Families will still wonder where their next meal will come from, or how they will pay the electric bill. Men and women will still search in vain for jobs.

The environment will continue to be violated. Creeks and rivers will still be clogged with waste and debris. Beauty will not return everywhere to these most beautiful mountains.

I know that our education system will continue to have major flaws, and will continue to struggle toward a brighter day. I know that many of our most talented young people will still leave us to pursue greener grass elsewhere.

Our churches aren't going to suddenly be filled to capacity with prayerful people. Politics won't become pure and perfect overnight.

I know it will take constant and determined vigilance to rebuild our spirit of community.

I know all of this and yet it does not make me cynical. I won't cry or wail. I won't be discouraged. I won't lay down at the end of the road and say, "I can't take another step."

Even though I know I cannot change all the pain and sorrow of Appalachia into joy and hope, I will never lose my own sense of peace.

I will keep hoping because this victory was never mine to win. I know this is too big a job for one man, or even one organization like CAP or the Church.

The only thing that can win this victory is the love, the wisdom, and the power of God.

As the last stage of my life comes rushing at me, and in the midst of crisis, I see hope everywhere. It is God in our lives.

I see young faces rising above the crowd. I see more hands raised in prayer. I see couples making commitments to each other with prayerful determination.

I see new people, new energy, new ideas.

The trail is not abandoned. It is full of people moving together toward God's goal.

I see faith coming from our churches. I see a new generation of religious folks entering the fray with their heads held high, their feet on solid ground, and their hands firmly committed to the work of God.

I see volunteerism on the rise, because there is a growing awareness that we are God's stewards and our highest potential is to be of service. I see many of those who have volunteered with us in the past helping the poor in the Philippines, in South America, in Africa. These people came here for a while, learned what service was and what could be accomplished with faith and community. They have taken those lessons and are applying them throughout all of God's earth.

I see more and more groups intent not so much on winning glory, but dedicated to working together with no fear of who's going to get the credit, or who's going to get the praise. As long as the work is done, as long as the people are helped, that's all they care about.

That's a new breath of hope in these hills and I see it growing in power.

I see Education questioning its past performance and wondering if we should be training our young people to solve problems and build a better society, rather than simply training them to get good jobs. In the past, I've worried about a focus that said, "Education is good because if you finish high school you'll get this kind of job. And if you finish college you'll get this kind of job."

I see a new awareness that education is valuable because it changes us and enables us to do God's work.

Recently, I spoke with a group of high school students who had dedicated themselves to volunteer work. In this small high school, the students had given nearly 5,000 hours of work in one year to places like hospitals, nursing homes, and agencies helping the poor. I was so heartened to hear these students say they wanted to do even more.

To my mind, these students have been educated in what it means to be a member of society. That is a good sign.

I also see good signs of a new era in politics. We still have too much corruption and too much selfishness and greed. Too many politicians still give in to the pressure of lobbyists. But I think that there are also men and women who have taken on a nobler task than to achieve power and prestige.

There are many seasoned politicians whose leadership is true. Many of them have helped us in our work over the years and I am inspired by them. I am impressed by what they've been able to do with the power given to them by the voters.

There are also young people who work for and with these veterans, who want to be part of a legacy and leave something worthwhile behind.

Another sign of hope is that I am also seeing more and more people willing to pray. People who want to truly live a prayerful life. They want to go beyond prayer on Sunday mornings, and make prayer a part of all their days and hours.

This is so important.

There isn't a problem that can't be solved, a bridge that can't be built, or a mountain that can't be climbed if we pray.

There isn't a heart that can't be moved if we ask for the help of God and His son, Jesus Christ.

We need to be like Peter on the mountaintop. When we see the glory of God we need to cry out, "Lord, it is good for us to be here."

We need that kind of enthusiasm. We need to say, "It's good to be here. Here with God!"

We need the charity and love of Christ. We need to be convinced that we can do all things in Him.

I know I carry my treasure in an earthen vessel, but I want to concentrate on the treasure, not the vessel.

I am glad I have had the chance to do God's work. I am glad to know that the struggle will continue after I'm gone because God keeps gathering His family here in Appalachia.

Where I have planted, others will water, and harvest . . . and plant the next crop.

I ask everyone who reads these pages to join me in the dream of changing a crisis into a blessing.

Pray with me. Offer your sacrifices with me. Work with me. Cry with me. Smile and laugh with me.

Jesus said, "Where two or more of you are gathered in my name, there am I in your midst."

St. Paul said, "If God is with us, who can be against us?"

I come to the end of this volume and I say, "Yes, there are crises. Yes, there are needs. Yes, there are tears and worries. But we have the greatest power of all on our side. How can we lose?"

To my heavenly Father, I say, "Thanks. I thank Your Son my Lord Jesus. I thank You for being a God full of love and devotion. I thank You for the chance that You gave me to do Your work here in Appalachia.

"I shall never give up, Lord. I shall try. I shall try.

"I shall never give up."

THE MOUNTAIN SPIRIT

Our bimonthly magazine, *The Mountain Spirit*, will keep you up-to-date on the work of the Christian Appalachian Project as we continue to help the people of this poverty-stricken area help themselves. In the magazine, you will also find moving, inspiring stories about the people we serve. If you would like to subscribe to this publication, please complete the order form below.

THE MOUNTAIN SPIRIT **Subscription Order Form**
Please send me CAP's magazine *The Mountain Spirit*.

Name_____

Address _____

City _____ State _____ Zip _____

Please return this Order Form to: Christian Appalachian Project, 322 Crab Orchard Street, Lancaster, KY 40446-0001.

If You'd Like to
Know More About the
Christian Appalachian Project . . .

For more information about CAP, or for
additional copies of *A Time of Crisis, A Time for Christ,*
please write or phone us at our headquarters:

Christian Appalachian Project
322 Crab Orchard Street
Lancaster, KY 40446-0001
(606) 792-3051

Thank you for your interest and support!

Volunteering With
THE CHRISTIAN APPALACHIAN PROJECT

☐ I am interested in volunteering for one year.

Please send information.

Name _____

Address _____

City _____ State _____ Zip _____

Please return this form to: Christian Appalachian Project, 235 Lexington Street, Lancaster, KY 40444. (606) 792-2219.